NORTHERN STEAM FINALE

Barrie Walker

First published in the United Kingdom in 1986 by
Jane's Publishing Company Limited
238 City Road, London EC1V 2PU

ISBN 0 7106 0375 4

Typeset by Netherwood Dalton & Co Ltd, Huddersfield
Printed by Netherwood Dalton & Co Ltd, Huddersfield

JANE'S

Cover illustrations

Front: The ex-LMS Jubilees operating from Leeds Holbeck
enjoyed an Indian summer, easily outlasting their sister engines at
other depots. No 45593 *Kolhapur* negotiates the points at Settle
Junction with the Bradford–Heysham parcels on 23 March 1967.
This engine is now preserved at Tyseley, and returned to main line
service in 1985, running on special workings in North Warwickshire.

Rear: 'Britannia' No 70013 *Oliver Cromwell* was again on railtour
duty in April 1968 and is seen leaving Kirkham with the second leg of
the 'Lancastrian No 2' special, which it hauled to Windermere and
Morecambe.

This page: The most expensive water of all time? Class 4MT
No 43130 delivers two cans of drinking water to the signalbox at
Settle Junction. The locomotive had brought the water all the way
from Rose Grove shed, to which it duly returned after making the
delivery. Ivatt's class 4MTs were affectionately known as
'Doodlebugs', and No 43106 is preserved on the Severn Valley
Railway at Bridgnorth.

Introduction

When I began to prepare the photographs for this book I would not have considered it to be a history book, but that is undoubtedly the final result.

Time has passed so quickly, and it is amazing to me that 20 years have elapsed since many of the pictures were taken. It therefore follows that many readers will be too young to have witnessed the great days of steam for themselves. Sadly, they missed a magnificent spectacle.

The 1950s and 1960s were, to me, the halcyon days of the railways, although older enthusiasts would probably disagree. My only regret is that I did not take up colour photography at the outset of this period, my early efforts being almost entirely black and white. Colour film was, of course, expensive, grainy and very slow, while few cameras had shutters capable of 1/500th of a second, or lenses faster than f3.5. I started to concentrate on colour slides in 1961, using a Super Paxette 2LT camera and Kodachrome film. However, in 1965 I graduated to a Leica M2, again using Kodachrome film, occasionally experimenting with the 'X' variety. These combinations of cameras and films, together with a Weston light meter, produced all the material presented in this portrayal of those final years.

Residing as I do in North-West England, it is quite natural that most of my slides depict scenes in that part of the country. My favourite location was, and still is for that matter, the Settle & Carlisle line, particularly south of Ais Gill. The ever changing patterns of light on the hills, the varying cloud formations, and above all the sights and sounds of the steam locomotives have given me many happy hours. It was unusual to meet a fellow photographer, and between trains conversation was generally conducted with the well-informed sheep and cattle by the lineside!

How things have changed. Nowadays a steam special over the Settle & Carlisle is guaranteed to produce traffic jams of enormous proportions on the normally quiet dales roads, while the fields overlooking the line tend to resemble the terraces at a football ground.

Railway photography has changed too. Automatic cameras, faster films, better and more varied lenses, and perhaps the dramatic increase in car ownership have all helped to contribute to the wealth of material being produced today. If only all these aids had been available 30 years ago.

Northern Steam Finale is an attempt to present the last few years of steam working, hopefully in a reasonably balanced manner, and to depict the changing railway scene. There are omissions, of that I am well aware, but I do hope that readers will find it a pleasurable publication.

In conclusion I would like to thank Ken Harris at Jane's for his considerable help in the preparation and presentation of this book, and also my long-suffering family, whose days out have frequently been interspersed with lineside visits in the most unusual and unattractive places.

BARRIE WALKER
Worsley, Manchester
January 1986

Left. Eight railway workshops and three private manufacturers were involved in building the members of the Stanier 8F class of 2-8-0s, although many of these were for War Department use overseas and never saw LMS service. No 48697, built at Brighton in 1944, is pictured near Llangollen on 29 April 1967 at the head of the RCTS 'Wrexham, Mold & Connah's Quay' railtour.

Above. Recently overhauled at Crewe, another Class 8F No 48765 simmers in the sunshine at Manchester Piccadilly on the afternoon of 28 April 1966. The permanent way gang is working under the wires in the former Eastern Region side of the station, previously known as Manchester London Road. This particular engine was built at Doncaster, one of 103 constructed by the LNER for its own wartime use.

Above. Following the failure of the booked engine on 5 June 1968, standard Class 4MT No 75027 was hastily summoned from Carnforth to work the ballast train from Swinden Quarry to Skipton. It arrived in the middle of the afternoon facing the wrong way, and is seen gathering its train in the snow-like dustiness of the quarry sidings on the former Grassington branch.

Right. Up with the Lark! On the very next morning Class 4MT No 75019 was beautifully turned out to work the same train down the branch. The 4-6-0 is pictured leaving the quarry at the more usual time of 7 am, bound for Skipton, before continuing over the now-closed section of line to Blackburn.

In February 1964 the 'Princess Coronation' Pacifics were still hauling occasional passenger trains on the West Coast main line, but this was only to continue for a short time. No 46240 *City of Coventry*, built at Crewe in 1940 and originally streamlined, rests on Crewe North shed after working in from Perth. Although many of the class were capable of first-rate work, and were definitely preferred by enginemen to the Standard 4-6-2s, they were all withdrawn in September 1964.

It was fitting that the last working Stanier Pacific was No 46256 *Sir William A Stanier, F.R.S.* The engine powered a return farewell special from Crewe to Carlisle on Saturday 26 September 1964, and was photographed on Crewe North shed the following day. Reflecting H G Ivatt's involvement in the design, No 46256 differed from the earlier members of the class in that it had a self-cleaning smokebox, self-emptying ashpan, rocking grate and modified cabplate, in addition to which roller bearings were fitted to all axles. The engine was named at Euston on 18 December 1947 by Sir Robert Burrows, Chairman of the London Midland & Scottish Railway, just two weeks prior to nationalisation.

Above. On 20 April 1968 the Stephenson Locomotive Society's 'Lancastrian No 2' rail-tour passes Sandylands on the Morecambe to Heysham line, headed by Class 5MT 4-6-0 No 45156 *Ayrshire Yeomanry*. This engine spent most of its working life in Scotland and was one of only four of the class to receive a name. It was finally withdrawn from Rose Grove depot during the week ending 10 August 1968, on the closure of that shed.

Right. Probably because of its spotless external condition and the fact that it was named, No 45156 was used on several railtours in 1968. Piloted by No 45073 at the head of a joint Severn Valley Railway Society/Manchester Rail Travel Society special in July 1968, the pair storm through the closed station of The Oaks, on the climb from Bolton to Entwistle.

Above. On a hot summer's day in July 1966, A2 Pacific No 60530 *Sayajirao* backs into Perth station before taking a mixed freight south to Edinburgh. Together with sister engine No 60532 *Blue Peter*, these were the last A2s to remain in service. Although both locos were in good condition, *Blue Peter* took the leading role, being constantly used on expresses and special duties. *Sayajirao* was withdrawn on 19 November 1966.

Right. A regular duty for *Blue Peter* was the 1.30 pm Aberdeen–Glasgow, and the engine was maintained in immaculate condition by Ferryhill shed. This train is pictured on the cliffs near Cove Bay, following the steep climb out of Aberdeen. At the time of writing the engine is preserved at Dinting, but unfortunately is not available for main line workings.

Opposite. The final version of the LMS 2-6-4 4MT tank was introduced by Charles Fairburn in 1945. No 42183, one of the batch of engines built at Derby some five years later, rests in the evening sunshine at Bolton shed in August 1966.

Left. Over the years the 2-6-4 tanks were used on semi-fasts and express duties throughout the London Midland Region. Here No 42587 blasts through Bromborough with the 3.25 pm Birkenhead–Paddington on 5 March 1967, only to fail on reaching Chester, having been worked too hard! This was the last day of steam working between Shrewsbury, Chester and Birkenhead, the final train being the 9.40 pm Birkenhead–Paddington, which was hauled as far as Chester by Class 5MT No 44690.

Left. Carrying out the work for which it was designed, ex-LMS 8F No 48191 trundles through Heatley & Warburton with a Stockport–Liverpool freight on an afternoon in April 1968. This 2-8-0 was built by the North British Railway Company in Glasgow in 1942.

Right. With its front numberplate removed, BR Standard Class 9F 2-10-0 No 92224 passes Long Preston box with a trainload of rails from Workington to Manchester in August 1966. This locomotive had a very short career. Constructed at Swindon in 1958, and originally allocated to the Western Region, it was withdrawn from Warrington shed during the week ending 30 September 1967.

Left. Long before the 'Cumbrian Mountain Express' had seen the light of day, the Settle & Carlisle line was well used for enthusiasts' specials. The RCTS chose this route for its 'Scot Commemorative' railtour in February 1965 when No 46115 *Scots Guardsman* hauled the train from Crewe to Carlisle, travelling via Chorley and Blackburn. The tour ran into near-blizzard conditions on the fells, but still managed to reach Carlisle. Here No 46115 pauses at Hellifield, whilst the tour party visits the former motive power depot, which at that time housed several engines destined for preservation. The yellow stripe on the cabside indicated that the engine was not allowed to work south of Crewe, due to the restricted clearances imposed by the 25 kV 50 Hz overhead electrification.

Above. At the northern end of the S&C, Holbeck 'Jubilee' 4-6-0 No 45562 *Alberta* waits to leave Carlisle with the Jubilee Railway Society's 'South Yorkshireman No 8' railtour of 7 October 1967. This class is well represented in the preservation stakes, there being three working examples and another which is likely to be used for spare parts.

17

Above. Rods removed and bound for the breakers' yard, Fowler dock tank No 47165 is seen at Bolton shed in October 1964. It had worked with sister engine No 47164 and the former Lancashire & Yorkshire Railway 0-6-0ST No 11305 as a shunter at Horwich Locomotive Works. Ten of these Fowler engines were built at Derby in 1928 and 1929, and incorporated a very short wheelbase to enable them to negotiate tight curves on dockland lines. In view of the final duties of Nos 47164 and 47165, it was perhaps ironic that the design work for the class was completed at Horwich.

Right. At Crewe Works steam locomotives were still used for shunting operations well into the diesel era, and indeed at the end of 1964 all the engines were repainted. Class 4F 0-6-0 No 44450, a development of a Midland design, is seen in the works yard sporting its works reporting number on a plate attached to the bufferbeam.

A very dirty Standard Class 2 tank No 84025 waits at Horwich with the auto train to Chorley in September 1965. Today it is difficult to imagine that there was ever a railway beyond the former Lancashire & Yorkshire Horwich Works, which is itself now closed. This train returned to Horwich from Chorley, and then worked forward to Bolton. Such was the volume of traffic that on this trip it was only placed in the platform road if a passenger arrived to board it!

Indicating a previous overhaul at Swindon Works, green-liveried Standard Class 5MT No 73035 prepares for turning at Shrewsbury depot in October 1964 before working back to Chester. Along with the Standard Class 4s and Stanier Class 5s, these engines bore the brunt of passenger and goods traffic on the line to Birkenhead prior to dieselisation. Built in 1953 and allocated to Polmadie depot, No 73035 hauled a railtour from Chester to Birkenhead on the final day of steam working, 5 March 1967.

Left. A Castle in Yorkshire. Restored to Great Western Railway livery, although now sporting a double chimney, No 7029 *Clun Castle* approaches York with a special from King's Cross to Newcastle on 9 September 1967. The 4-6-0 had taken over the train at Peterborough and was detached on the King Edward Bridge at Newcastle, being prohibited entry into the platform at Central station due to insufficient clearance. The train was taken into the station by Class K1 No 62005, as pictured on page 47.

Above. Great Western engines were regular visitors to Crewe on both freight and passenger turns, the locomotives usually being serviced at Crewe South shed. 'Hall' 5MT 4-6-0 No 4959 *Purley Hall* leaves Crewe with a freight for Shrewsbury on 26 February 1964.

23

Right. In 1936-37 the Manchester Collieries purchased five former North Staffordshire Railway tank engines from the LMS, and these were put to work on the Walkden system of colliery lines. The last survivor, 0-6-2T *Sir Robert,* hurries along in fine style at Linnyshaw Moss, at a point where part of the M61 motorway has since been constructed. This engine was built at Stoke in 1920, as one of the 'New L' type, and carried the number 72.

Opposite. At the hub of the Walkden system, National Coal Board J94 0-6-0 *Stanley* (No 3302 of 1945), built by the Hunslet Engine Company, storms up the steep bank past the works with the regulation 10 wagons of coal from Astley Green Colliery. These would travel via Ashtonfields Colliery and Linnyshaw Moss sidings (where the picture opposite was taken) before being picked up by a BR engine for the journey down to Kearsley sidings on the Manchester–Bolton line.

Left. During the final months of steam working, railtours traversed almost every route in Lancashire, and many engines were specially cleaned by enthusiasts to work these trains. One such, former LMS Class 5 No 44888, heads a Roch Valley Railway Society special near Kenyon Junction, on the Manchester–Liverpool line.

Above. For some time Class 5MT No 45305 had been kept by Springs Branch shed for special workings, including Royal Train pilot duties at Parkside. It was used on the 'Lancastrian' railtour of 6 April 1968 and is seen here leaving Burscough Bridge for Southport. The engine was subsequently sent to Drapers of Hull for cutting up, but it remained intact and after some considerable time was restored to working condition; it is now named *Alderman A E Draper*.

OVERLEAF

Left. By August 1966 only some 150 of the 733 War Department 2-8-0 locomotives remained in service. No 90482, formerly No 63131, was in reasonable mechanical condition when it was photographed between Long Preston and Hellifield whilst working a Carnforth–Leeds freight. None of the BR engines was preserved, but the Keighley & Worth Valley Railway eventually managed to obtain a similar one from abroad. The last three members of the class were withdrawn from Normanton depot on 30 September 1967.

Right. Also photographed from the bridge carrying the A65 road over the railway, Stanier 8F 2-8-0 No 48743 ambles northwards out of Hellifield with the Brindle Heath–Carlisle mixed goods on 20 August 1966. This engine was another of the 8Fs built at Darlington and Doncaster for wartime service on the LNER, returning to the LMS in 1946-47. The building in the far distance is the former Hellifield motive power depot.

27

Above. The first Standard Pacific, No 70000, emerged from Crewe Works early in 1951 and was named *Britannia* at Marylebone on 30 January by the then Minister of Transport, the Rt Hon Alfred Barnes. The engine was withdrawn in June 1966, but can still be seen working on the Nene Valley Railway at Peterborough. Looking in superb condition, No 70000 was photographed at Crewe in September 1964.

Right. When the remaining 'Britannias' were withdrawn at the end of 1967, No 70013 *Oliver Cromwell* was retained for special workings. The Pacific hauled the 'Midland Centenary Special' on a Derby–Manchester–Nottingham diagram in June 1968, and is seen here between Edale and Hope on the return leg. This engine also powered the famous '15 Guinea Special', heralding the end of steam on BR, between Manchester Victoria and Carlisle on 11 August 1968, before running light to Norwich for private preservation at Bressingham.

Whisky Galore? Many people only remember Sir Nigel Gresley for his express passenger engines, but perhaps surprisingly he was also responsible for several freight designs, including the J38 of 1926. Hopefully, the crew had not gone for a 'wee dram' as No 65901 basks in the sunshine at Markinch with the Thornton Junction crane, outside the John Haig whisky distillery.

Pick up freight. Thompson B1 No 61132 shunts at Milnathort, on the line from Perth to Dunfermline. Prior to the Beeching axe, most country stations had a small yard or siding served by a daily freight service. Sadly these rapidly disappeared, and by 1965, when this picture was taken, many had already gone.

Left. Brakevan railtours were very popular in the days of steam, and on a cold day it was not unusual to see a train with smoking stovepipes, as the occupants of the vans lit fires to keep warm. This was not the case on 20 August 1966 as Ivatt Class 2MT No 46517 passed White-gate, on the former Cheshire Lines Committee Winsford & Over branch, in perfect summer weather, with the repeat LCGB 'Cheshire Cat' tour.

Above. No 47202, one of the Midland Railway's condensing 'Jinties', is pictured at Agecroft depot on the evening of 22 April 1966. The engine had worked the LCGB 'Cotton Spinner' railtour around Manchester the previous weekend, hence the reporting number 1T55 chalked on the smokebox rim. This was a Johnson design of 1899, which was later rebuilt with a Belpaire boiler, and 39 of the class were fitted with condensing apparatus for working in the London area. No 47202 was the last survivor of this batch, being withdrawn with the only remaining non-condensing engine, No 47201, from 17 December 1966.

In the days of steam most freights and many passenger trains were banked up Grayrigg. The Grayrigg bankers buffered up at Oxenholme and dropped off as the train approached the top cutting, after climbing the 7·1 miles finishing with a gradient of 1-in-106 over the final 2 miles. Here Standard Class 4MT No 75041 drops off the rear of a northbound freight in October 1967. This engine was scrapped at Cohens of Kettering in 1968.

Right. On a lovely evening in June 1967 Class 5MT No 45268 hurries south at Brock on the West Coast main line with a train of wire coils. The trees which were planted on the M6 motorway embankment have grown considerably, and the road is no longer visible from this vantage point. The overhead wires have also spoiled an excellent location for photography.

Above. Squally showers with intermittent sunshine greeted the ex-Lancashire & Yorkshire 'Pug' No 51218 at Shawclough, on the former L&Y Rochdale to Bacup branch, on 19 February 1967. The engine hauled three brakevan specials, sponsored jointly by the Roch Valley Railway Society and the LCGB, between Rochdale and Whitworth. Final closure of the line took place on Saturday 19 August 1967, when the last train ran to clear the branch of rolling stock. Part of the line near Healey Dell viaduct has now been incorporated into a nature trail. No 51218 is preserved on the Keighley & Worth Valley Railway.

Right. An April 1967 brakevan tour over the Cromford & High Peak line produced two clean J94s, Nos 68006 and 68012 of Buxton shed. The pair start the climb from Longcliffe to Friden on a blustery afternoon.

In the shadow of Pen-y-ghent. Running nearly two hours late and making heavy weather of the climb from Settle Junction to Blea Moor, 'Britannia' No 70031 *Byron,* in filthy condition, struggles northwards with the 'Thames-Clyde Express' The 'Britannia' was deputising for the usual 'Peak' which had failed further south. Note the roof-level nameboard on the first coach of the train.

On the roof of England. Amidst the wonderful scenery of the fells, Ivatt Class 4MT 2-6-0 No 43139, built at Doncaster in 1951, stands on the up main line at Dent whilst permanent way gangers lift the track from the up sidings. The photograph was taken from the down signal bracket (with the permission of the District Engineer) on 25 August 1966.

Left. Lostock Hall was the last BR shed to operate main line steam locomotives on the BR system. This view of the depot, taken from the road bridge, shows its general decline by the summer of 1968. The last engine to be withdrawn from Lostock Hall was Stanier Class 5 No 45110, which is now preserved on the Severn Valley Railway at Bridgnorth and named *RAF Biggin Hill*.

Above. Latterly the Standard Class 5s fitted with British Caprotti valvegear were concentrated on Patricroft shed before its closure on 1 July 1968. Here No 73138, showing definite signs of wear and tear, awaits its next turn of duty in April of that year.

Below. Tender first in the Irwell Valley. Only four months of steam operation remained when this shot was taken at Clifton in April 1968. No 44947, cleaned unofficially by enthusiasts at Bolton shed, threads the woods with an Ashton Moss–Horwich freight. Bolton depot closed on 1 July 1968.

Right. Bunker first in the Conway Valley. Stanier tanks Nos 42574 (built by North British in 1936) and 42644 (built at Derby in 1938) pass the signalbox at Betws-y-coed on the return trip from Blaenau Ffestiniog to Llandudno with the LCGB's 'Conway Valley' railtour of 24 September 1966. No 42574 shows the rivets clearly on the tank sides and is unlined, while No 42644 is fully lined out in BR black livery.

Left. On the Eastern side of the Pennines the A1 Pacifics disappeared very quickly, but a few were retained for freight and standby duties. No 60156 *Great Central*, unfortunately with nameplates and crest removed, is undergoing minor repairs inside the straight section of York shed in the summer of 1965. Two A1s, Nos 60124 and 60145, survived into 1966, with No 60145 *Saint Mungo* hauling the final East Coast farewell to passenger steam special from York to Newcastle and back on 31 December 1965.

On Saturday 9 September 1967 *Clun Castle* made its run from Peterborough to Newcastle (see page 22), but it was not allowed into Central station because of restricted clearance. After photographing the 'Castle' at York, I caught the following express northwards, and as we approached Newcastle the special had just changed engines on the King Edward Bridge. No 62005, also later to be preserved, was provided to work the train the remaining few yards into the platform. It was spotlessly turned out by Tyne Dock shed and fitted with a suitably inscribed, if gaudy, headboard. The engine later took the empty stock to Heaton carriage sidings before the train returned south behind *Flying Scotsman*.

Highland Elegance. The Scottish Region of British Railways was quick to recognise the potential of steam specials hauled by unusual or preserved engines. Accordingly, between 1959 and 1961 GNSR 4-4-0 No 49 *Gordon Highlander*, NBR 4-4-0 No 256 *Glen Douglas*, the Caledonian Single No 123, and the Highland Railway Pioneer 4-6-0 No 103 were all repainted in their respective pre-grouping colours and put to work. Over the Easter weekends in the early-1960s all four engines could usually be seen at work. Here HR No 103, the 'Jones Goods', in its distinctive yellow livery, leans on the curve at Corkerhill shed after working the 'Scottish Rambler No 4' tour of 17 April 1965.

6 March 1965 saw the use of preserved LNER K4 class 2-6-0 No 3442 *The Great Marquess* on the Stephenson Locomotive Society/Manchester Locomotive Society 'Whitby Moors' tour. This was one of a class of six constructed at Darlington in 1937 as a development of the K2/2 class. They were specially built for the West Highland line in an attempt to reduce double-heading, and later became prototypes for the highly successful K1s. The engine is seen at Wakefield Kirkgate before setting back onto the train, and the gentleman in overalls alongside is the proud owner Lord Garnock. In 1985 this engine was undergoing overhaul on the Severn Valley Railway.

Above. Black Five – Black Smoke. The Saturdays-only Sheffield – Morecambe storms through Settle Junction behind Class 5MT No 44943 on 22 July 1967. This engine was allocated to Leeds Holbeck; it was withdrawn on 30 September 1967, at the end of the summer timetable.

Right. The highest station in England was also miles from the village it served. When asked why the station was so far from the village, one of the locals is reputed to have said, "Happen they wanted it near't railway". Another filthy Class 5MT, No 44844, runs through Dent with a Bescot–Carlisle goods in August 1966.

Below. The ungainly-looking 'Crab' was introduced in 1926 as a Hughes LMS design, built under the direction of Sir Henry Fowler. No 42715 was one of the few still active in Yorkshire when it was photographed at Normanton in August 1965. The doubtful honour of being the last working 'Crab' fell to No 42942 (pictured opposite), following withdrawal of the remaining four from Birkenhead shed in December 1967.

Right. The LCGB's 'Conway Valley' railtour enters Rhuddlan, on the Rhyl–Corwen branch, hauled by No 42942 on 24 September 1966. The passenger service on this branch was withdrawn in three stages, the section between Rhyl and Denbigh (including Rhuddlan) losing its scheduled passenger services on 19 September 1955.

With nameplates removed and in unlined green livery, Standard Pacific No 70012, formerly *John of Gaunt*, sets back into Crewe station from the south to take the Epsom Railway Society's special forward to Wolverhampton on 3 April 1966. The locomotive was involved in an unusual incident at Ilford in August 1957 whilst hauling a Liverpool Street–Norwich express, when the coupling pin between the engine and tender sheared, allowing the tender and train to break away. Following this occurence, modifications were made to the drawbar and braking systems, there having been no easy method of bringing the engine to a stand after the tender had become detached.

In November 1955, 'Britannia' No 70026 *Polar Star* was derailed at Milton near Didcot, when working up from South Wales to Paddington. In the report on the accident it was stated that the view forward from the footplate had been restricted by the smoke deflector handrails. Over a year later the Western Region 'Britannias' were modified at Swindon, having their handrails removed and extra handholds cut in the deflectors. This alteration is clearly visible as No 70015 *Apollo*, one of the engines concerned, leaves Rose Grove with a tour of Lancashire in March 1967.

Left. Like many other industrial systems, the Manchester Ship Canal Railway was severely curtailed over the years and by 1967 was but a shadow of its former self. MSC 0-6-0T No 67 takes a welcome break whilst working a farewell brakevan tour through Trafford Park in August of that year. Built by Hudswell Clarke as No 1397 of 1919, this engine is now preserved on the Keighley & Worth Valley Railway.

Below. Bradford Corporation sewage works at Esholt was the location of two oil-fired steam locomotives which shunted a rather unusual design of wagon on a short but steeply-graded line. 0-4-0ST *Nellie*, built by Hudswell Clarke as No 1435 of 1922, puts up a fine smoke screen at the Esholt Works.

19 July 1966 saw Class 5 No 44703 deputising for A2 No 60532 *Blue Peter* on the 1.30 pm Aberdeen–Glasgow as the A2 was undergoing minor repairs. The crew of the Class 5 seemed intent on keeping time as the train thunders out of Aberdeen on the climb to Cove Bay. This engine had obviously been overhauled in Scotland, indicated by the larger smokebox numerals.

The streamlined Gresley A4s were the pride and joy of the East Coast main line from the day they were built until the diesels took over. Engines in good condition were then transferred north of the border to continue their sterling work on the Glasgow to Dundee and Aberdeen services. Here No 60034 *Lord Far-* *ingdon,* the last of the class, enters Perth several minutes early with the 8.25 am Glasgow–Aberdeen in July 1966. Due to the early arrival, the location left a lot to be desired, and the pole sprouting from the chimney was a masterpiece of timing!

59

Above. LMS 'Jubilee' 4-6-0 No 45574 *India* stands quietly on shed at Carlisle Kingmoor in October 1964. Many years earlier I was almost sick of the sight of this engine as it hauled expresses between Blackpool and Manchester through my local station. I was surprised to find it in such good condition, although the shed staff appear to have been a little enthusiastic with the sand. O that it were still hauling those expresses today!

Right. Another 'Jubilee' 4-6-0, No 45742 *Connaught*, leaves Carlisle Citadel for the long climb to Ais Gill with the 4.37 pm stopping train to Bradford in the autumn of 1964.

Left. One of the last regular steam passenger workings was the 12.17 pm Preston–Manchester Victoria, being the last leg of the train's journey from Glasgow. The usual motive power was a Lostock Hall Class 5, generally in indifferent mechanical condition. No 45350 has steam to spare as it freewheels downgrade through the autumn leaves at Clifton with the train in October 1967. This train was still steam hauled as late as March 1968, but for some obscure reason only on Mondays!

Above. Polished until nearly black, GWR 'Manor' No 7802 *Bradley Manor* battles out of Shrewsbury with the down 'Cambrian Coast Express' in October 1964. This was the last Western Region titled express to remain steam-hauled, although only between Shrewsbury and Aberystwyth, and Aberystwyth shed retained a few 'Manors' especially for this duty. They were always immaculately turned out, often sporting white buffer heads and smokebox door hinges.

Evening Shadows. A variety of motive power
was used for the RCTS 'Wrexham, Mold &
Connah's Quay' railtour of 29 April 1967 (see
page 2). Running very late, Standard Class 9F
2-10-0 No 92058 pauses at Neston North, with
the low evening sun highlighting locomotive
and train.